How To Make Surfboard

A Complete Guide To Build, Shape, Wax And Repair Your Surfboard

Copyright@2023

Lazar Adonis

1

Table of content

CHAPTER ONE

Instructional Guide To Make A Surfboard

The creation of a surfboard calls for a significant amount of persistence, accuracy, and, of course, resources. It is easy to make errors since this procedure is laborious and takes a long time. On the other hand, if you put in the effort, you will be rewarded with the satisfaction of having a surfboard that is fully original and one-of-a-kind since it was built according to your requirements and specifications.

Items You Need

- Three fluorescent lights (if shaping in a room)

- Safety goggles

- Very thin plywood

- Marker

- Wooden workhorse

- Jigsaw

- Finger sized planer

- Thick pencil

- Surfboard blank

- Surfboard resin and catalyst

- Hand planer

- Steel mesh 4 inches by 4 inches (10 cm x 10 cm)

- Fiberglass cloth (at least 6 oz. or 168 g, however the heavier the cloth the stronger the board will be, 20 feet or around 6 meters is recommended)

- Scissors

- Electric planer

- 3 plastic squeegees

- Masking tape

- Fiberglass rope (39 inches or 100 cm)

- Surgical latex gloves

- 3 wide paintbrushes

- Electric drill with a drill-bit with a diameter of 1.33 inches (3.4 cm)

- Small knife

- Electric circular sander

- Hot coat resin and catalyst

- Leash plug

- Surgical facemasks

- Sandpaper suitable for the electric circular sander (both coarse and fine)

- Dust brush

- Wet sandpaper

- Fin box and fins

Part 1-Constructing The Surfboard

1-Choose an appropriate workplace, such as a garage or a workshop.

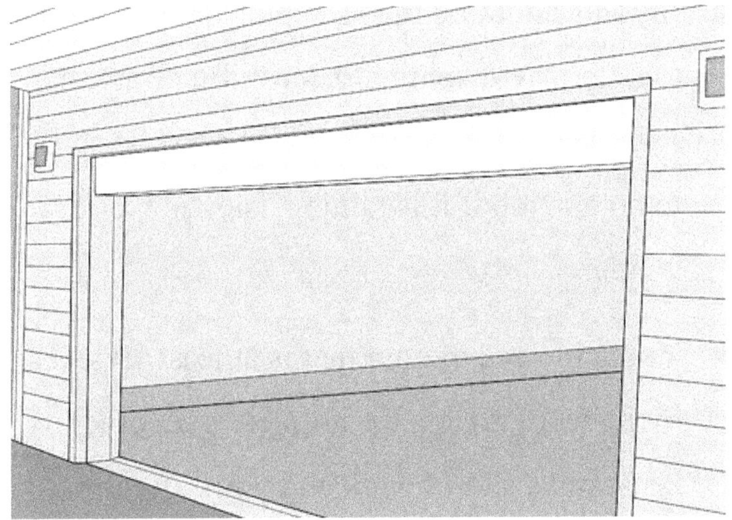

You will want a room that is not just spacious but also has enough air circulation. You are going to create a mess, therefore you need to ensure that the location you choose can accommodate it.

- When it comes to ventilation, working outdoors is preferable; but, an indoor facility with three precisely positioned fluorescent lights will highlight defects in your shape, allowing you to identify and correct them at an earlier stage.

- If you want to do this task outside, you need to keep an eye on the forecast. Be aware that regardless of the weather, you won't be able to do any job if it is raining, snowing, or even windy.

- You will need a room that is at least 10 feet by 8 feet (3 meters by 5.4 meters) in order to construct a short board, and you will need a room that is longer than 10 feet in order to construct a long board. It is possible that it would be a good idea to construct a room that is dedicated solely to the construction of boards.

2-Acquire a slender piece of plywood and make a template for your board by tracing the outline of a surfboard onto it.

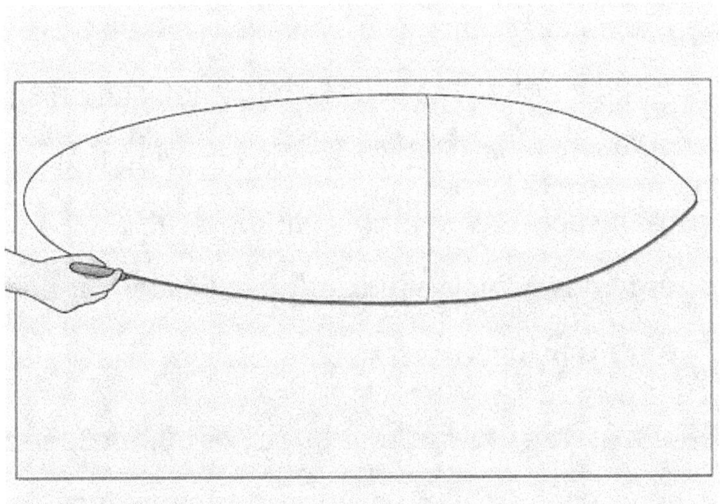

You should test out a few various surfboards until you locate one that you like and then replicate its design. Place the surfboard on top of the plywood that you have already laid out on the ground, and then use a marker to trace the board's shape.

- Ensure that the stringer, which is the wooden strip that runs the length of the board across the centre, is properly aligned between the ends of the plywood.

- You may make it simpler to trace by marking placement points with a marker at the nose and the tail, at the board's midpoints, and then all the way around the board, ensuring that each successive point is parallel with the previous, which will result in an exact cut-out of the surfboard.

- While you are working on the outline, you must exercise great caution not to move either the board or the plywood.

3-Attach the plywood to a workhorse and use a jigsaw to cut it to the desired shape.

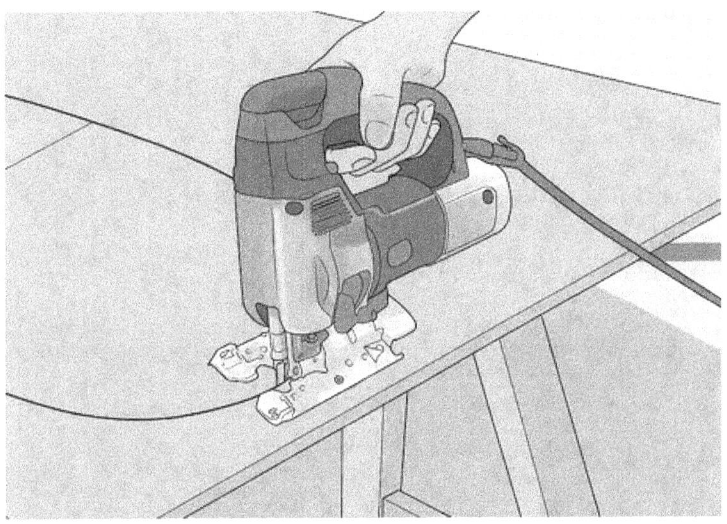

Put on your goggles for protection, and then turn on the jigsaw. When creating your surfboard-shaped template, be sure to cut following your pattern with extreme caution.

● When you are ready to cut through the plywood, make sure the edges that you will be cutting are dangling over the sides of the sawhorse, and use a blade made of carbon steel.

4-Go to a store that sells surfboard supplies and purchase a blank surfboard made of foam or wood.

The foundation of each surfboard is something called a "surfboard blank," which is what you will mold into the finished product. Your own choice will determine whether you go with foam or wood.

- Blanks for surfboards come in a wide variety of dimensions, including weight, length, density, and form. How you ride the wave will determine the sort of blank that is necessary for you. If you want to ride smaller waves, you should look for a blank that has less density (as long as you are okay with having to replace it more often). The denser the board is, the greater its strength and the longer it will continue to function for.

- EPS foam is often acclaimed as a suitable option of material for the blank since it is both a sturdy and long-lasting material and also has a lower density than polyurethane foam. This combination of qualities makes it a popular choice for the blank.

Part 2-The Process Of Shaping The Surfboard

1-Place the blank piece with the bottom facing up on the workhorse, and trace the pattern onto it.

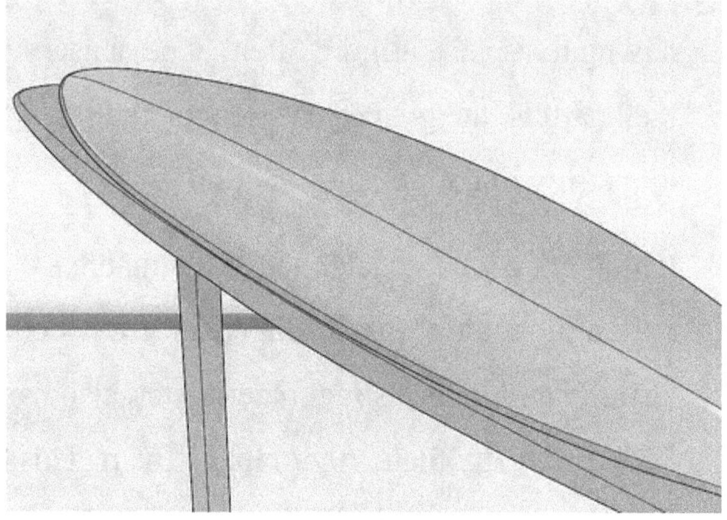

Place the template on top of the blank, making sure it is entirely flat along the stringer line, and then go to the next step. Using a thick pencil, transfer the outline of the surfboard template onto the blank, moving from the nose to the tail of the board. Flip the blank over and trace the outline of the shape onto the front of it.

- If you have never shaped a surfboard before, you should spend some time at a surfboard workshop and see how the professionals do it before you attempt to shape your own board. This will give you a better sense of the way and manner the shaping procedure works.

2-Using the jigsaw, trim away any extra foam (or wood) that is on the surfboard blank.

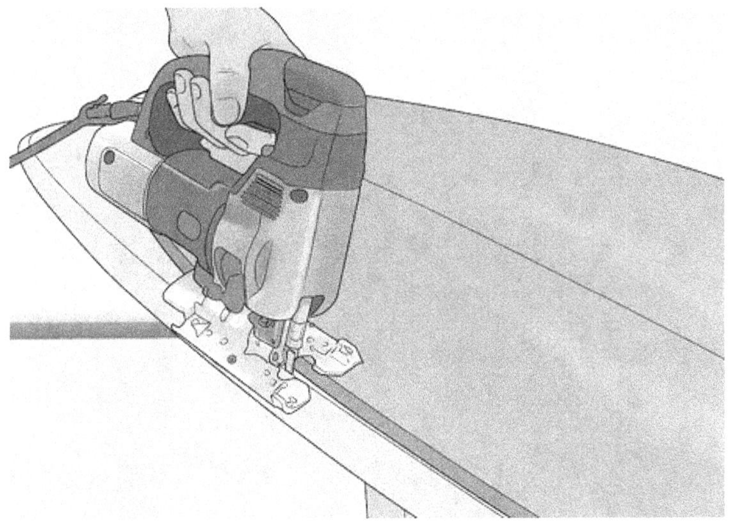

Be careful to allow an excess of one to one and a half inches (2.5 to 3.81 centimeters) from the trace of the surfboard template. This will give you space to shape the board.

- Use considerable care during sawing, particularly when cutting around the stringer on the snout of the log.

3-Clamp the surfboard blank to the workhorse and plane both sides of the board while it is still attached.

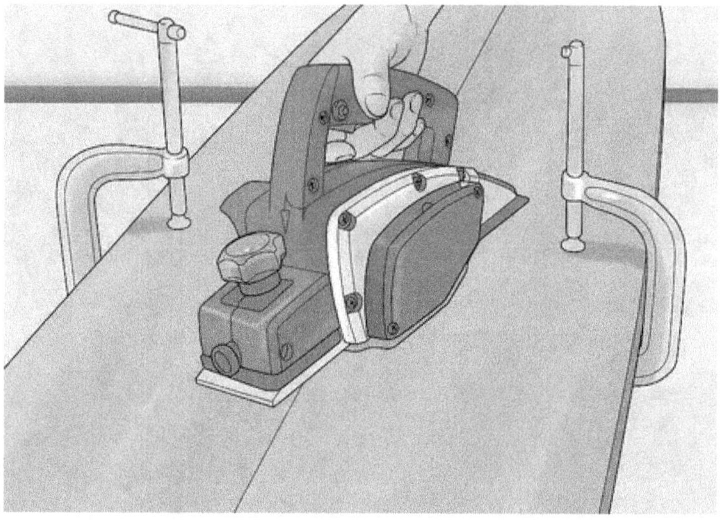

Plane the bottom of the board very carefully using an electric planer set to a depth of.08 inches

(two millimeters) moving from the tail to the nose
of the board. Flip the board over and plane the
surface that will be facing up. Plane just enough
so that you can get to the softer white foam that
lies behind the more rigid surface.

- When you approach closer to the nose, it will
  be hard to utilize the electric planer; thus, you
  should switch to using hand and finger
  planers for more accuracy at this point in the
  process.

- You may purchase all of the necessary planers
  from a home hardware store or a shop that
  specializes in carpentry supplies.

4-Using a hand or finger planer, give the curvature of the rails the desired shape.

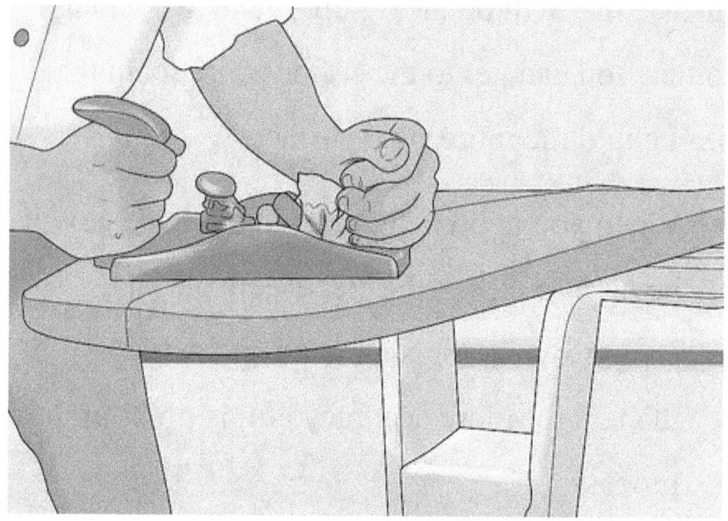

The curved sides of the board are called the rails, and the way you shape them will determine how well the board rides and turns. Construct a curve that is flatter for increased buoyancy in waves with less energy, and one that is steeper for improved performance in waves with higher energy.

- The rails of your board may be shaped in an infinite number of different ways, but generally, the gentler the curve, the more forgiving your board will be. More frequently than not, boards with better performance will have sharper curves.

5-Using steel mesh, smooth up the rails of the blank that you have.

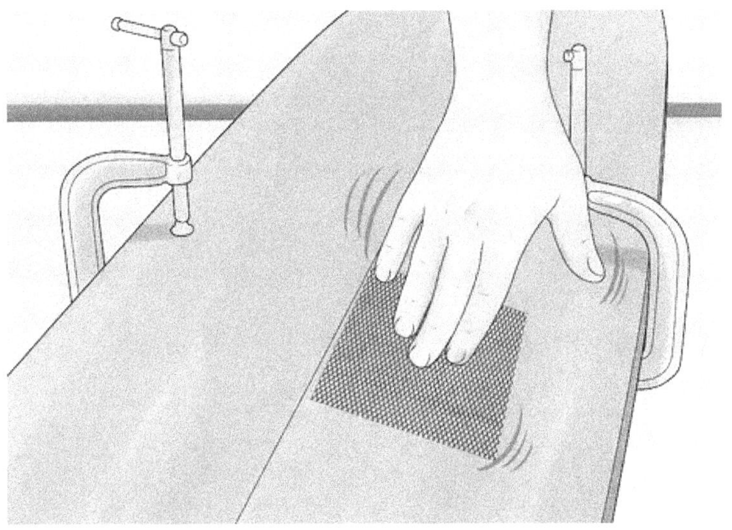

Slide a piece of the steel mesh from the tail to the nose using both of your hands as you move it along the rails. Alter the rear one-fourth of the rail to have a more acute edge, while the front three-quarters should have a more rounded appearance.

Part 3-Putting Resin On The Surfboard

1-Coat the bottom of the surfboard blank with a layer of fiberglass cloth that weighs 6 ounces (168 grams).

Make sure that you leave around two inches (five centimeters) of excess material draped over the board after you have trimmed the cloth around the contour of the blank using sharp scissors. You will need to fold the fabric over the rails, so cut the material into "V" shapes along the curves of the board.

- A fiberglass shop, a maritime supply shop, or a surfboard supply shop are some of the places you may get fiberglass fabric.

2-Mix the catalyst with 24 ounces (800 mL) of the resin.

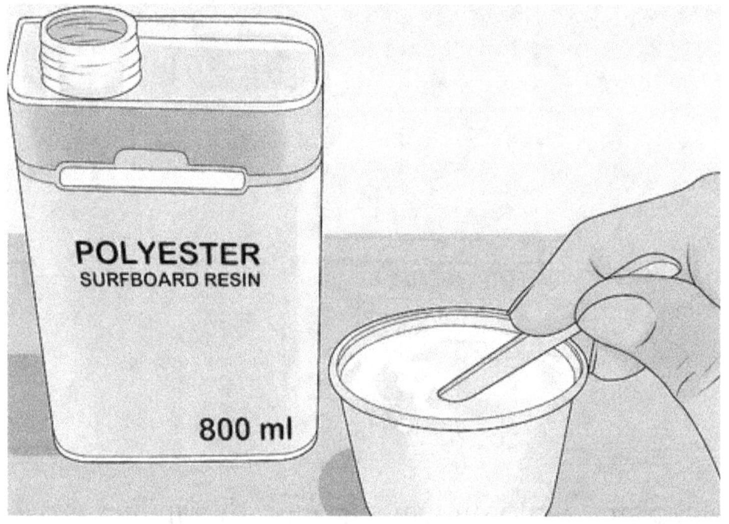

Resin and catalyst are the two components that, when combined, will result in the formation of a transparent and brittle covering on the surfboard. After looking up the appropriate ratios for the product you are using, combine all of the

ingredients in a bucket or a small plastic
container.

- A surfboard supply shop is the place to go to
  get polyester surfboard resin and catalyst.

**3-Pour the surfboard resin mixture over the
fiberglass fabric, and then spread it out so that
it is uniformly distributed.**

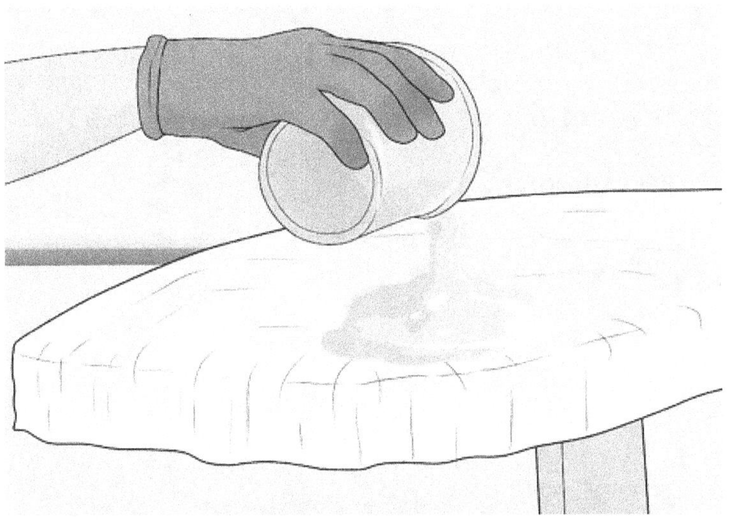

Using a squeegee, spread the resin in a figure 8
pattern over the centre of the board, starting in the
middle of the board itself. When you approach

the edges, you should work the resin so that it goes out and over the rails to secure the fiberglass.

- Timing is critical since it should take around five to six minutes for the resin to cool down. Make sure that the entire piece of fabric is thoroughly soaked and that it is firmly attached to the blank. Leave any leftover cloth (it will be covered gradually), but be careful to squeegee away any excess drips that have accumulated.

4-After giving the resin time to harden for about a day, you should repeat the process on the other side.

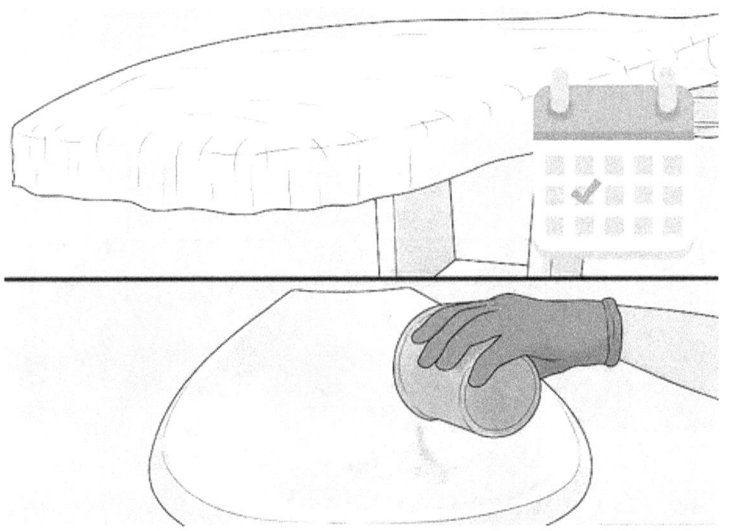

You should apply the resin to the upper side using the same way that you used for the bottom. To increase the deck's level of durability, apply an additional layer of fiberglass cloth weighing 4 ounces (133 milliliters).

Part 4-Adding The Fins

1-Go to a surf supply store and get a detachable molded fin system for your board.

The ideal solution is to go with a system that can be removed, since this will allow you to take the fins off when transporting your board. Rather of making your own fins, it is considerably simpler to purchase ones that have already been formed.

- If you want to be able to vary the positioning of your fins on your board depending on the waves, you may also add several fin positions to your board.

2-Make a mark indicating where the fins will go, then trace their boxes.

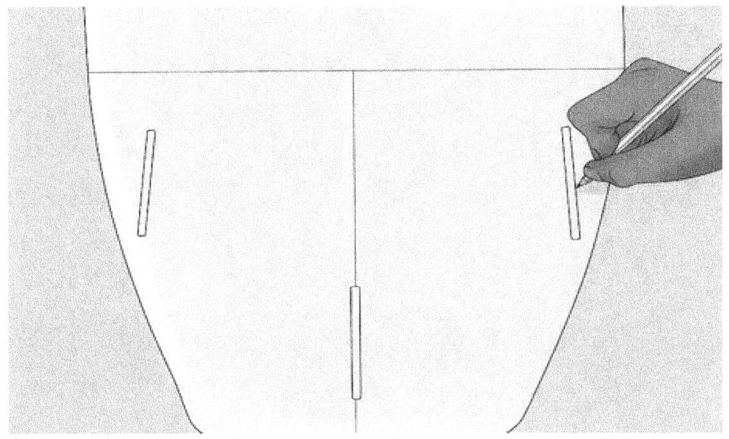

Take measurements using the surfboard that served as your pattern, and then use a marker to make a mark on your new board indicating where the fins will be placed. Make a drawing of the fin boxes' contours onto the board at the location where you intend to place them.

- The fin boxes are the component of the detachable molded fin system that are permanently installed in your board; the fins slide in and out of these.

3-Carve out shallow holes for the fin boxes using a chisel and sandpaper.

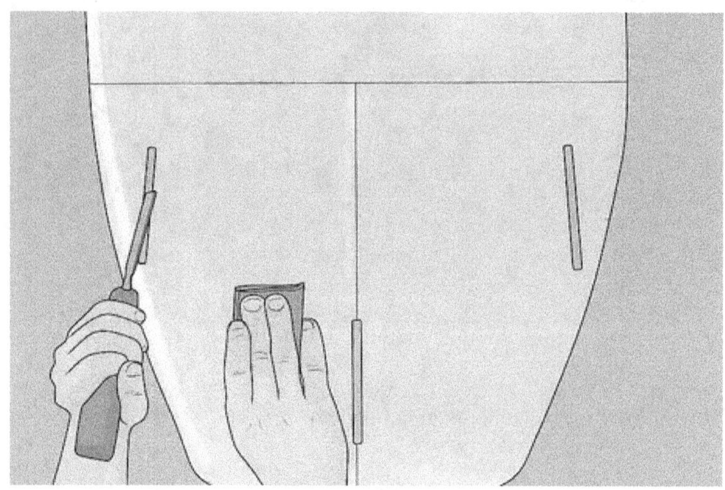

This step is optional. Take your time and carefully remove the innermost part of the fin boxes' outlines with a chisel. You just need to go in far enough for the fins to sit flat with the board. Sandpaper should be used by hand to make the holes smooth.

- Take care not to remove any of the material that lies outside of the contours as you are carving. First, use the chisel to remove the majority of the center section, and then, using the sandpaper, complete the final shape of the hole.

- You may pick up a chisel at a hardware store or a shop that specializes in building supplies. You could also use a sharp flathead screwdriver if you don't have a chisel handy.

4-Use surfboard resin to permanently fasten the fin boxes to the board.

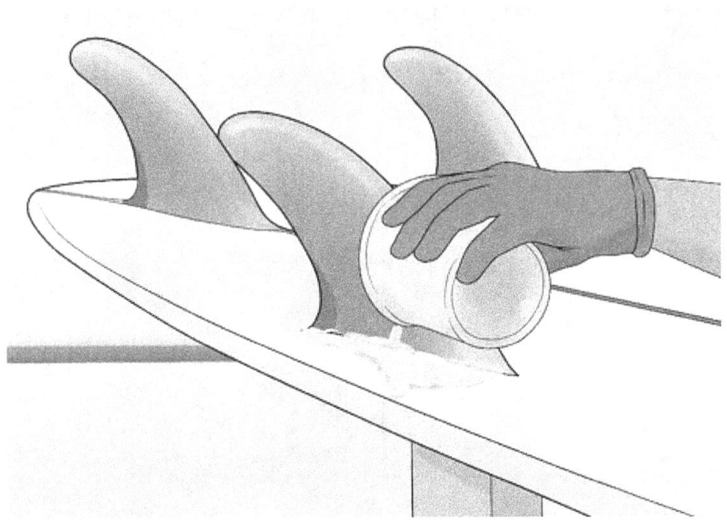

Just the right amount of resin should be poured into the holes to secure the fin boxes. After the fin boxes have been positioned such that they fit snugly in their holes, any extra resin should be wiped away around the sides.

- When you apply a layer of hot resin to the whole board, the fin boxes will become even more stable and solid in their positions.

5-Combine thirty ounces (one thousand milliliters) of heated resin with the catalyst, and then distribute the mixture all over the surfboard.

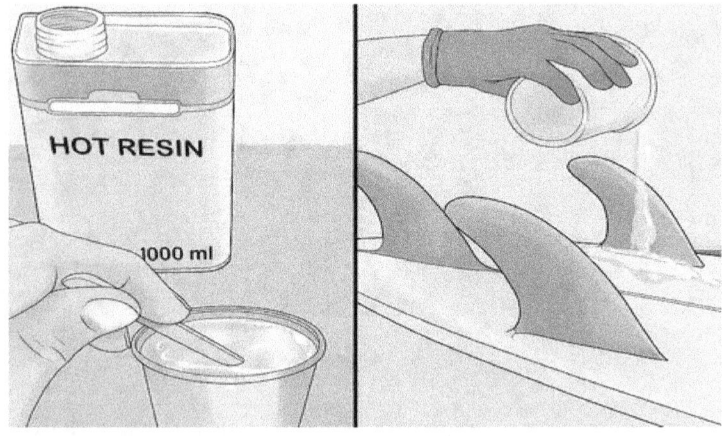

After turning the surfboard over so that the fin boxes are facing upward, pour the resin over the top of it and use a large paintbrush to spread it about until the whole surface, including the fin boxes, is coated.

- Take special care not to get any resin into the slots of the fin boxes, since this might prevent the fins from fitting properly.

6-After the resin has been allowed to dry for three hours, cover the opposite side of the board.

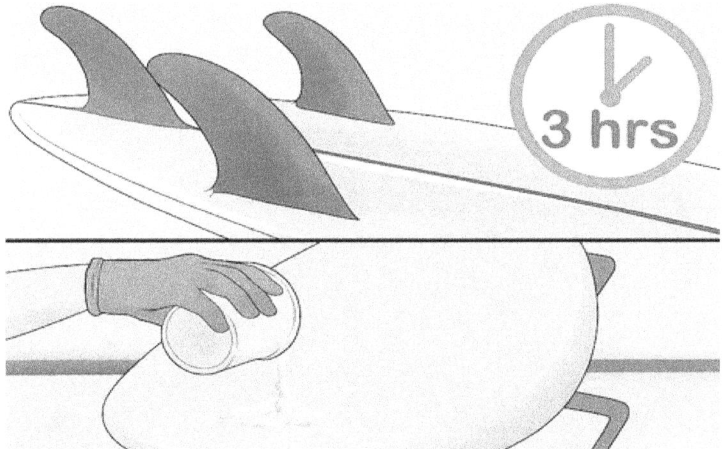

After the resin has had time to harden, turn the board over and carry out the procedure again for the top side. Be cautious to clean up any drips so that you do not end up with resin streaks on your board.

● Before doing anything further to the board, you must ensure that the top side of the resin is allowed to cure for a period of three hours.

Part 5-Sanding And Installing The Leash Plug

1-Using a drill bit with a diameter of 1.33 inches (3.4 cm), begin drilling a hole for the leash plug.

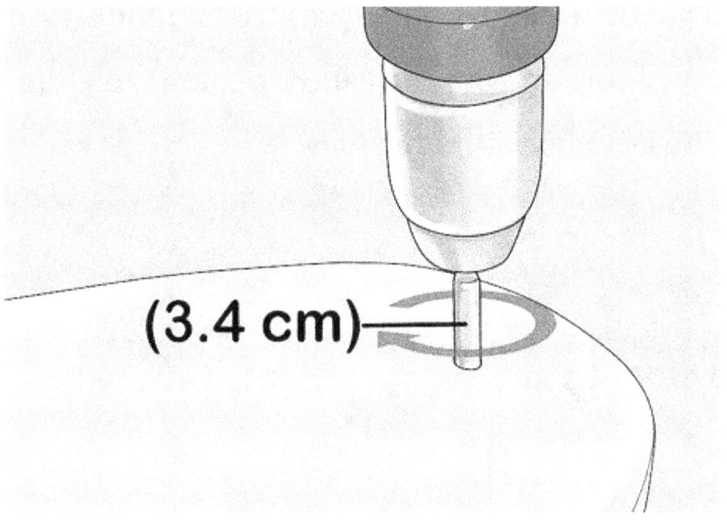

The hole that you drill has to be two and one quarter to three and one quarter inches (or six to eight centimeters) from the tail, close to the stringer. Make the leash plug flush with the deck by using a tiny knife to carefully scrape away the fiberglass and foam until it is.

- Your ankle leash will remain attached to your surfboard thanks to the leash plug. You may acquire one at a store that specializes in surfing.

2-Mix three ounces (one hundred milliliters) of hot coat resin with the catalyst, and then pour a little amount into the hole.

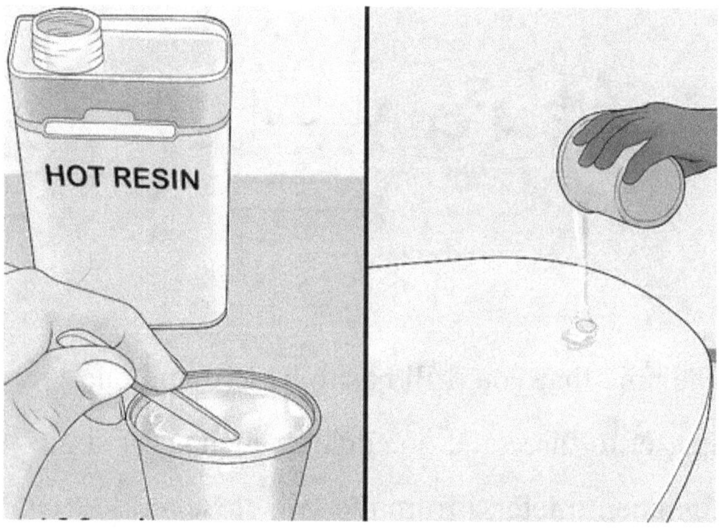

After inserting the plug for the leash into the hole, complete the setting process by filling the remaining space with resin. Use a paintbrush to remove any excess resin from the surface.

3-Sanding should not begin until the resin has been allowed to cure for at least one day.

After 24 hours, the leash plug will be completely fastened to the board, and the resin will have had enough time to cure. You will now be able to sand your board and finish it when you have completed this step.

4-Using an electric sander, smooth the surface of the surfboard's bottom side.

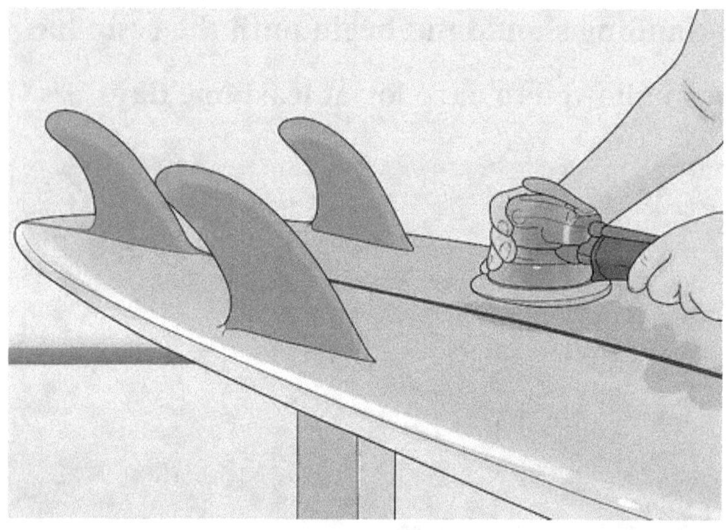

Sand the surface with sandpaper with a fine grit until all the irregularities and lumps are removed along with the sheen. Sand by hand any spots that are challenging for the electric sander to access.

- Sanding the board more than necessary will result in it being damaged. In the event that this occurs, patch the damage by using a little quantity of surfboard resin and a piece of fiberglass cloth, and then re-sand to smooth out any flaws.

5-Apply water to sandpaper with an extremely fine grit, and sand the board until it acquires a glossy appearance.

You won't be able to remove the finish if you use sandpaper with a very fine grit, but you will be able to polish it. Sand it until it is completely silky to the touch and glistening all throughout.

- If you skip this further sanding process, the board you're using will cause your skin to become inflamed and itching.

6-Let your board sit idle for a period of three days without being utilized.

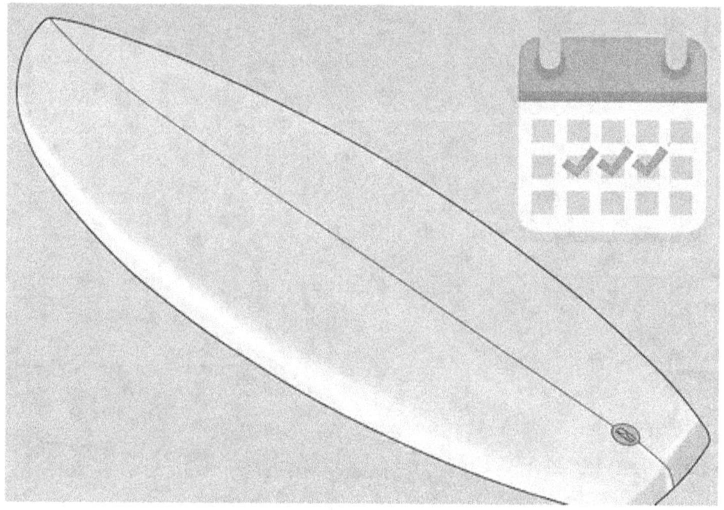

To conclude the procedure, you need to give the surfboard resin ample time to thoroughly harden. After a period of three days, your surfboard will be in a state of readiness to be used.

CHAPTER TWO

Instructional Guide To Shape A Surfboard

Premade boards that have just emerged from the manufacturer may be seen in surf stores. But what if none of them are suited to either your body type or the way you ride? The vast majority of beginning surfers are completely unaware that they may really participate in the manufacturing process of their very own surfboard. Making your own surfboard is not only a lot less expensive than purchasing one already made, but it also enables you to control every curve and angle of the board, which results in a ride that is more tailored to your own preferences. However, the shape of the board is the single most important factor in deciding how it will behave in certain situations. Although it does need a sharp eye and careful handling, shaping a surfboard is not nearly as difficult as one may initially believe.

You need to have a mental picture of the type of board you want to make, the appropriate set of tools, and the patience to sculpt the board bit by bit.

Items You Need

- Surfboard blank

- Sandpaper block

- Safety goggles

- Reformer

- Work table or rack

- Straight edge or T-square

- Electric power planer

- Handsaw

- Soft lead pencil

- Protective earmuffs

- Respirator

Part 1-Cut The Board Into Its Basic Shape

1-Get together all of the essential instruments.

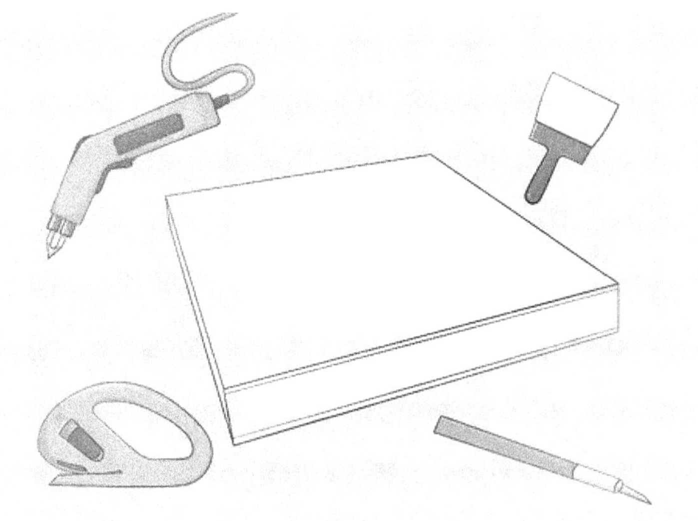

The suitable workspace as well as the necessary tools are required in order to shape a surfboard. Establish your workspace in a well-lit, open place with a table or rack that you may use to support the board while you work on it. You will be using a handsaw, an electric power planer, a surform tool, and a sandpaper block to shape your board. Additionally, you will be using an electric power planer. When doing measurements, having a pencil with a soft lead and either a straight edge or a T-square will be helpful as well.

- For the sake of your own personal safety, you should make sure that you are wearing a respirator, as there will be a significant amount of foam dust in the air once the process of shaping has begun. Additionally, you should make sure that you have eye and ear protection on (woodworking glasses or lab safety goggles and a pair of noise-deadening earmuffs will work perfectly) and that you have eye and ear protection on.

2-**Begin with a blank slate**.

You will need to have all of your basic supplies prepared before you can get started. The core of a surfboard is constructed out of lightweight foam, which is then trimmed to the appropriate dimensions by large manufacturers. The "blank" is a chunk of foam which has been cut into a rough surfboard shape and may then be shaved down to the surfer's chosen specifications after it has been shaped by a rider who is shaping his or her own board. This option is available for riders who want to shape their own boards. Buy yourself a blank and then start to work!

- It is recommended that you pick a blank that is larger than the size that you want your completed board to be. This will provide you more leeway when it comes to cutting and shaping the foam on the board.

- Surfboard blanks may be shaped in a matter of hours, and the process only costs a fraction of what it would cost to buy a readymade board.

3-Start by drawing the outline.

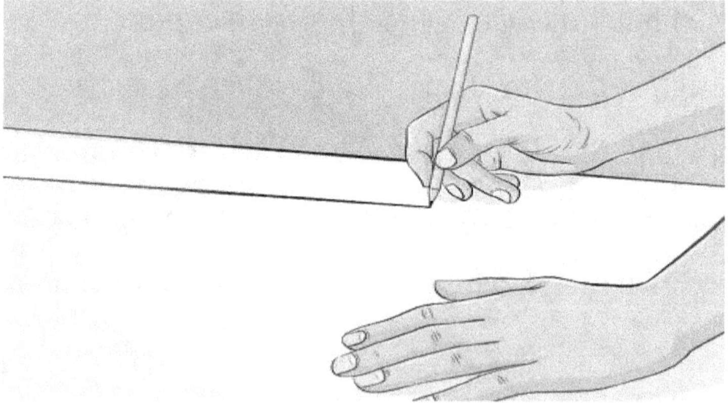

Make a decision about the general outline of the surfboard you intend to build. It may be a short performance board with a broad, rounded tail and shallow rails, or it could be a longboard with a pointed nose and a longer length overall. You may either utilize an existing surfboard that rides well as a reference or look out example dimensions for the sort of surfboard you want to build online and use those. Make a drawing on the rough foam blank following the outline of the board form you like most. In order to get the form of the board just perfect, you might find it helpful to utilize a template or some other kind of visual aid.

- When selecting a shape for your surfboard, make sure to pick one that takes into account your own characteristics and requirements. Your weight, body type, riding technique, and the type of surf you often ride may all have an effect on the length and form of the board you choose to ride.

● If you have an surfboard that you admire and you want to utilize it as a template, all you have to do is trace around it onto a few pieces of posterboard that overlap each other, and then cut out the outline. While you are cutting the blank foam surfboard to the desired length and width, place this outline on top of the blank.

4-Make the desired cuts in the board.

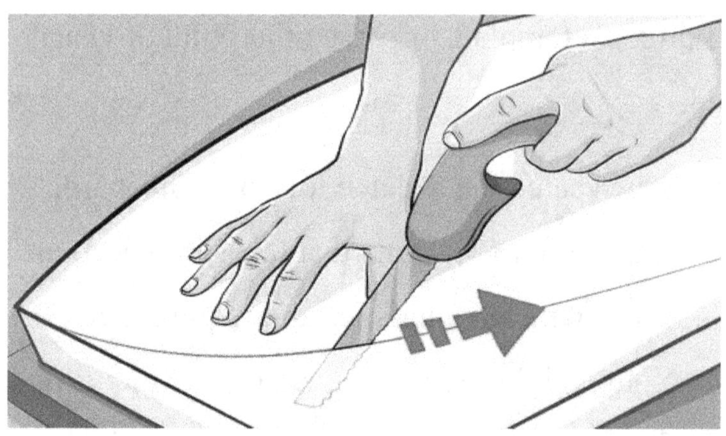

Use a handsaw to cut all the way around the outline you just sketched, beginning at one end of the shape (the nose or the tail) and working your way along each edge in turn. Strokes that are slow and smooth are the best way to prevent getting off track or tearing the foam. You don't need to worry about being really accurate because you'll be cutting and shaving the board as you go along.

- Securing the board on your work table or rack (some shapers utilize special racks with built-in adjustable clamps, while others use bungee cords or straps, or try to hold the board down with their free hand) will prevent the board from moving around while you are cutting it. Some shapers use special racks, while others simply hold the board down with their free hand.

**5-Sand the perimeters/edges until they have a
level surface.**

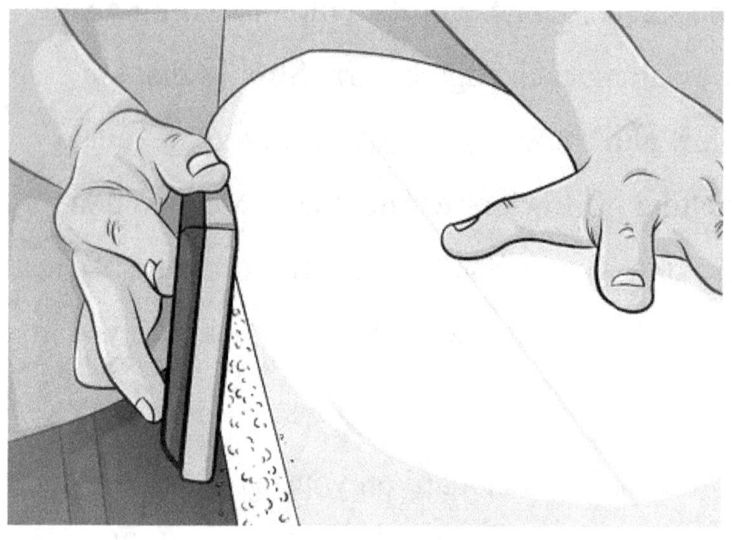

Smooth down the rough edges of the foam blank
by running a sanding block along the perimeter of
the blank. You want the edges to be as flat and
even as you can get them since they will serve as
the starting point for shaping the rails, which will
ultimately determine how the board rides and
behaves. From here on out, you'll be bringing out
the completed form of the board by employing
techniques that are more refined.

- Work out any imperfections caused by sawing the outline with the sandpaper provided in order to complete the task.

- The sides of the board should make an angle that is as close to 90 degrees to the deck (which is the top) and the belly (which is the bottom) as is possible.

Part 2-Contouring Of The Board

1-Reduce the height of the foam until it is the desired thickness.

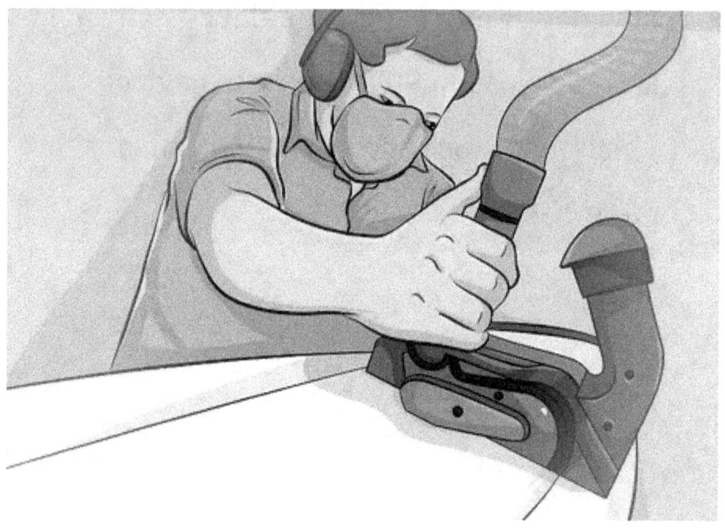

Connect the power cord to the planer, then adjust the depth setting to the desired level. To remove one thin layer of foam at a time from the exterior of the blank, pass the planer over the surface of the blank. Continue this procedure, making sure that you are continuously going back over the surface in the same way, until the board reaches the desired thickness or width.

- To prevent over-shaping or mistakenly removing an excessive amount of foam at once, set the depth gauge on the power planer to a shallow setting if you are just starting out with the shaping process.

- Mow the blank foam using motions that are smooth and straight. Instead of moving the planer in a straight line down the length of the board, begin at the stringer (the line that runs through the middle of the board) and guide it outward from the centerline. Because of this, the distance the planer needs to travel is reduced, which results in a smoother and more uniform shaving.

2-Adjust the rocker to your liking.

You are now able to begin adding "rocker,"
which refers to the upward curvature of the board,
as the board is now the appropriate thickness and
shape. To do this, remove some of the foam from
the area at the board's nose or tail (or both, if you
choose), so that the board's end curves upwards
ever-so-slightly. It is recommended that you keep
the blank a bit thicker at the ends since the
formation of the rocker will need you to remove a
significant amount of foam.

- You can make an effort at this with the power planer, but it could be simpler to use a surform tool since it will offer you more manual control over how much foam you remove and will protect you from making mistakes that are impossible to fix.

- Nose rocker prevents the front end of the board from sinking into the water as the surfer drops in, while tail rocker gives the rider the ability to control the rear end of the board for easier turning and shifting.

3-Carve a concave into the underside of the board.

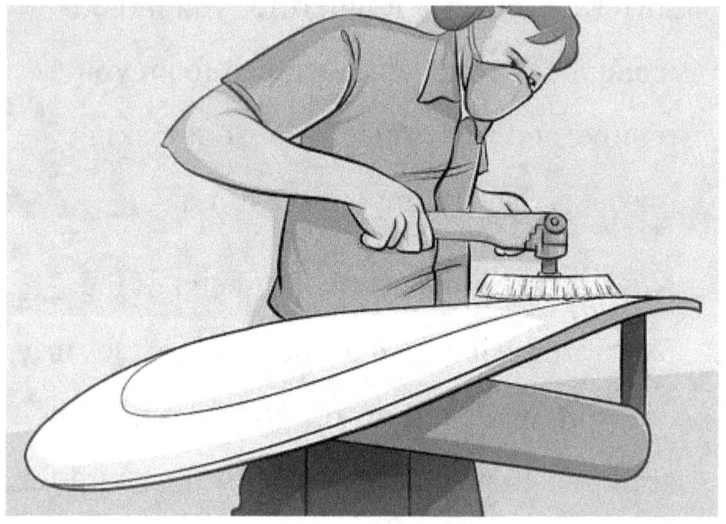

Concave should be added as the last touch to the deck's form. Concave is a phrase that is used to describe the way the bottom of the board folds inward toward the rider in order to catch the wave. When you have determined whether you want a deep or shallow concave, you may use the surform tool to carve farther into the belly until you reach the desired degree of concave.

- The concave shape of the board helps the surfer get traction by "cupping" the water and making it simpler to dig in.

- Concave surfboards inherently sacrifice some speed and lift due to the fact that their rails sit a little lower in the water than those of other types of boards.

4-Form and blend the rails as desired.

The rails, which are the board's outer edges, should be rounded off and shaved down as the final stage in the process of shaping your surfboard. Make a bevel on the straight edge of the blank's outline by using the surform tool to scrape away material until you reach the desired depth. Carry out the identical action on both of the beveled edge's sides at the place where they meet. To finish the rails, go over them with the sanding block and try to make the slope as smooth and gradual as you can.

- When shaping the rails of their surfboards, the vast majority of professional surfboard manufacturers employ a method known as "rail bands." The primary purpose of rail bands is to provide as a guide for shaping the board's rails so that they meet the deck and belly of the board with a smooth transition between the two.

- Crouch down frequently while you are shaping the rails so that you can inspect the board when it is at eye level. You will be able to identify any discrepancies in thickness or slope with the aid of this.

Part 3-Determining The Shape That Will Best Fit Your Board

1-Do not round the bottom of the object.

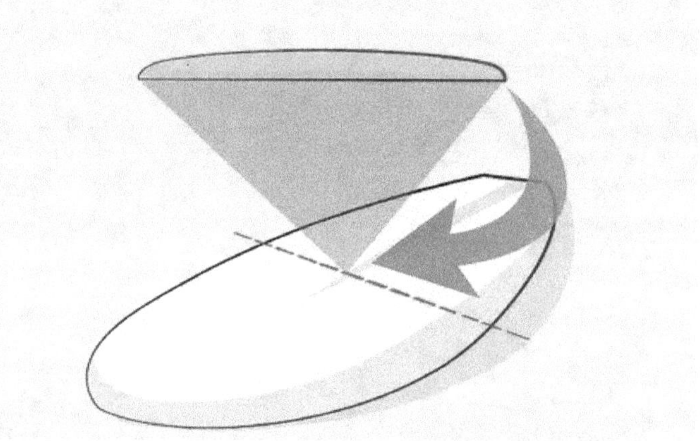

Surfboards with flat bottoms provide a bigger surface area for gliding over the water, which results in increased speed as well as improved balance. Because of their greater point of contact, they are also more stable while riding in heavy waves. Flat bottoms are versatile and perform well with many different types of surfboards. They are especially helpful in conditions where the waves are moving quickly and smoothly.

- Flat-bottomed surfboards have a greater surface area, which prevents the board from sinking into the water as much. This is an advantage for heavier surfers, who may benefit from using such boards.

- Before moving on to more specific contours, it is best to begin with a flat board so that you can acquire a sense of what you like and don't like about the board.

2-Give it a single, centered concavity.

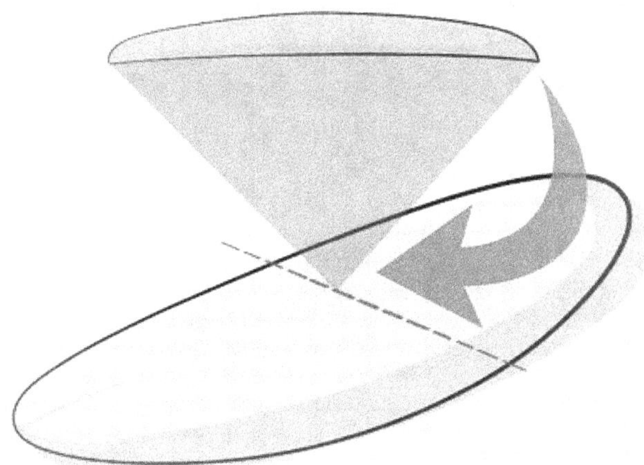

A single concave board has one big upturned curve located on the underside of the board. This helps the board to be more hydrodynamic since it can adjust to the shape of the waves and it makes it easier for water to travel below. Concave boards are excellent for performance because the rails sit lower in the water and give greater "grip" for the rider.

- A deep single concave is the preferred shape for many professional surfers' boards.

- In waves that are very rough or chaotic, single concave boards could be challenging to control.

3-Stick with the tried-and-true double concave shape.

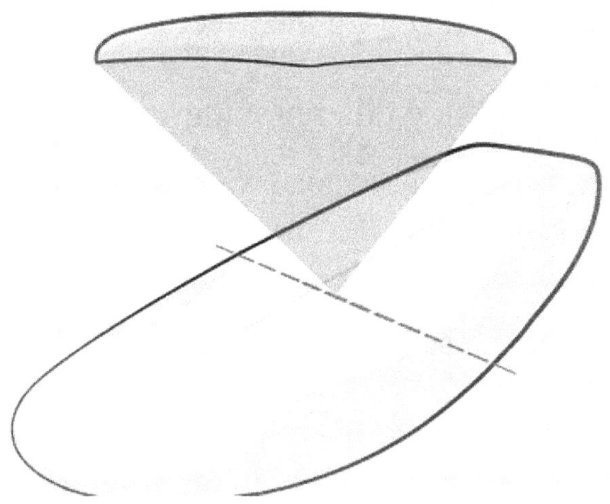

When viewed in cross section, double concave surfboards have a shallow "M" form due to the upward curvature on both sides of the stringer. If you purchase a readymade board right off the shelf, there is a good probability that the body contour of the board is double concave. The double curve makes the board more aerodynamic and generates lift, which enables the surfer to remain more on top of the wave.

- The lift and controlled channeling provided by double concave surfboards make them an excellent choice for less experienced surfers who are still getting their feet wet.

- When working on improving your balance, a rocksteady double concave board is the best tool to use.

4-Try making a "Vee" Shape.

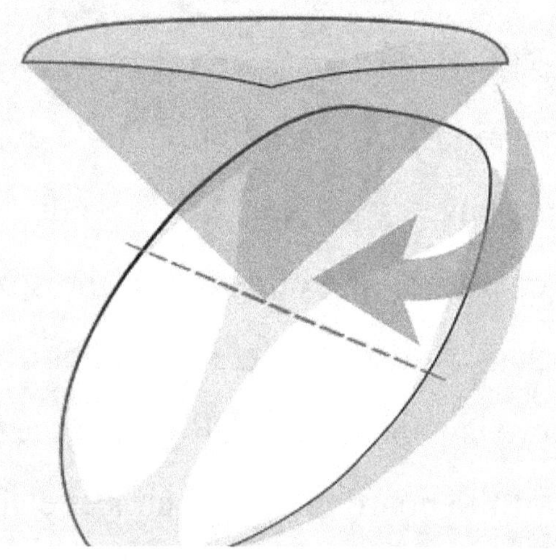

The name of this form of board comes from the angled point that is located on the bottom of the board. The Vee shape, which is comparable to double concave boards, offers the rider increased leverage for carving and quickly altering the direction they are going. The convex belly cuts through the water, which enables it to go quickly and makes it simple to control, all without causing the rider to lose their balance.

- If you regularly switch the position of your feet when you ride, a board with a vee form can be helpful for you.

- This is a common body posture for large wave surfing because it improves the rider's ability to balance finely, steer, and maintain stability.

CHAPTER THREE

Waxing A Surfboard: The Basics

Wax is an important component of a surfboard because it confers both grip and traction on the rider. A surfer has a substantially greater risk of falling off their board when there is no wax on it. Because of this, the appropriate application of wax may be the difference between successfully riding a wave and falling off the board. In point of fact, waxing a board is a rather easy and uncomplicated process. In this post, we are going to discuss how to apply the appropriate basecoat, then how to apply the appropriate topcoat, and finally how to comb it up.

Items You Need

- Surfboard

- Soft, cool, or tropical water wax

- Base coat wax

- Wax comb

- Denatured alcohol (optional)

- Plastic scraper (wax combs frequently contain a flat edge that will work all right)

- Wax remover (optional)

Part 1- Application Of The Basecoat

1-Start by applying your basecoat.

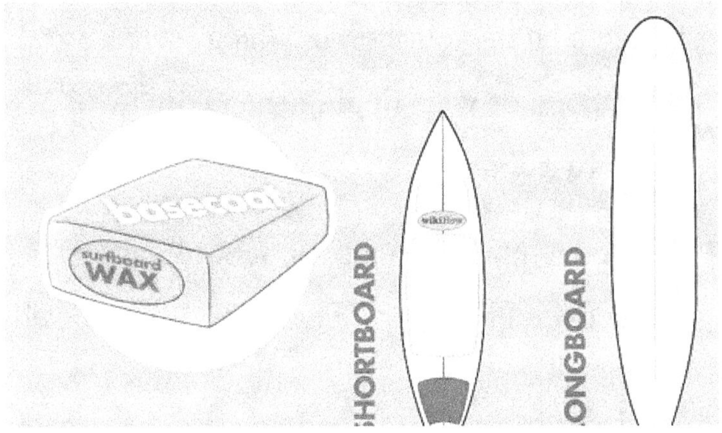

If you are using a longboard, wax the whole top surface of the board, beginning at the nose and working your way toward the tail. If you are

riding a shortboard, you should wax the topside
of the board from the front logo to the rear edge
(which is about two thirds of the board's length)
and from edge to edge.

- You won't be able to get by without a
basecoat wax, but the wax you use won't last
as long without it. If your board does not have
the correct basecoat, the topcoat will not
attach to the board. This will leave you with a
bare patch on your board, which increases the
likelihood of you slipping and sliding while
you are riding it.

- It is recommended that you leave your
basecoat on the board until you have rewaxed
it. The topcoat adheres strongly to the
basecoat you used.

2-When applying the basecoat, you may choose to use any one of numerous different methods.

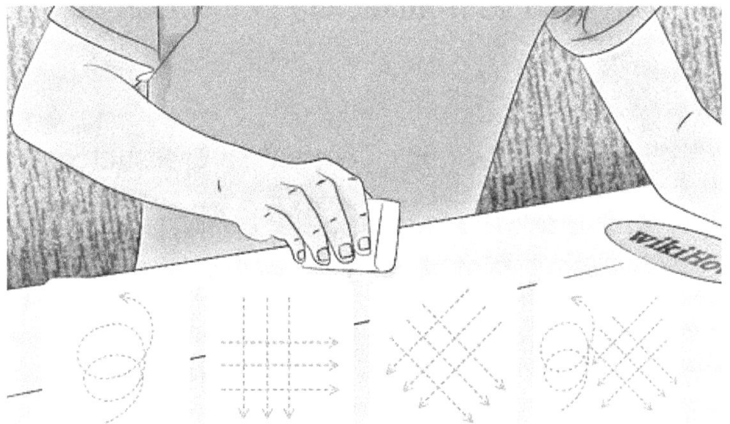

When it comes to getting the basecoat to attach to the board, surfers often utilize a variety of approaches, sometimes one at a time and sometimes in combination, including the following:

● Rub the wax into the board in tiny circles, going up and down the board until bumps begin to appear. The name given to this pattern is known as the circle pattern.

- Using a *straight line pattern*, rub the wax into the board in lines that are perpendicular to the rocker and go from the top of the board to the bottom.

- *Crosshatch pattern*: To create a crosshatch pattern, rub the wax into the board first in a diagonal direction, and then in a direction that is perpendicular to that diagonal.

- *Kitchen sink:* Rub the wax into the board in whatever direction you choose, utilizing any of the patterns described in the previous paragraphs or coming up with your own.

3-Continue to apply the basecoat until bumps appear in the surface.

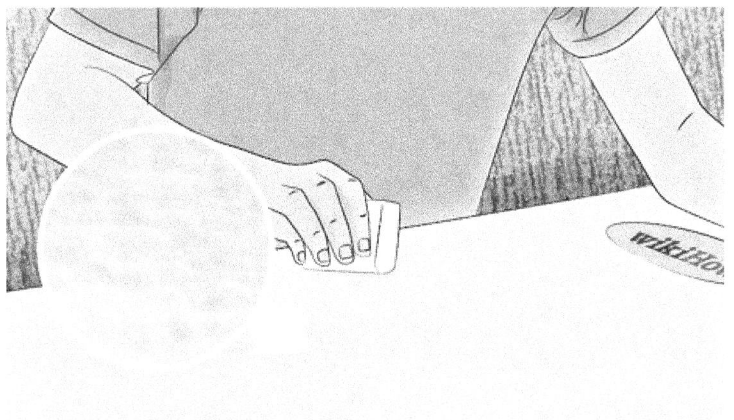

Instead of using the flat side of the wax stick, use the edge of it. Use right up until there is a rough covering on the surface. These bumps won't prevent your topcoat from sticking to them. It is possible that you may need to use a full stick of wax, or perhaps up to two sticks, in order to get the basecoat just perfect. This will be determined not only by the length but also by the width of the board.

Part 2 -Applying Of The Topcoat And Finishing Up

1-Start by applying your temperature-specific wax.

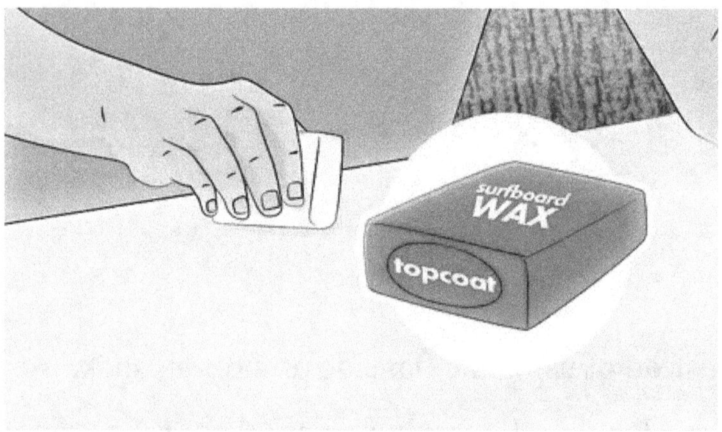

Apply wax all over the region that you just finished priming and painting with base coat. Rub the edge of the wax onto the board in tiny circles ranging from 3 to 6 inches (7.6 to 15.2 cm) in diameter, or use any of the other methods described in the previous paragraphs.

- If you want to err on the side of caution, consider applying a topcoat wax of a different color than the basecoat. If the color of your topcoat wax and your basecoat wax are the same, it will be more difficult to determine where you have applied the wax; hence, you should be careful to only wax in one direction if this is the case.

2-Give the wax a good comb.

To remove the wax from your board, run your wax comb through it. To rough up the wax and improve your grip on the board, run the comb in diagonal crosshatch lines. This will help you to hold the board more effectively. Ensure that you

pull it through the whole of the wax that is on the
board.

- If you haven't recently applied a fresh topcoat,
  you should use the wax comb on every single
  surf session. Wax may sometimes become flat
  and lose part of its grip, and this can happen
  from time to time. If you do not want to apply
  a fresh layer of topcoat, take the side of your
  comb that has the comb on it and create a
  crosshatch pattern by scraping in a diagonal
  direction.

3-Apply a little misting of lukewarm water all over the board.

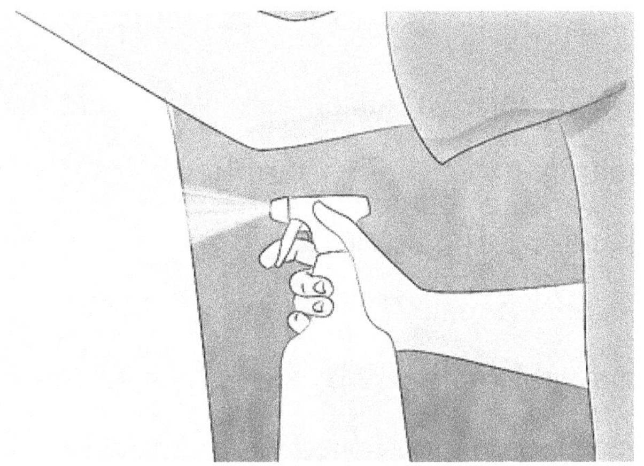

This will cause the wax to become more rigid and improve its ability to adhere to the board. You may now begin your surfing career in earnest.

CHAPTER FOUR

Instructional Guide To Fix A Surfboard That Has Cracks In It

The majority of surfers are aware that their boards may sustain a significant amount of damage throughout a day spent riding the waves, despite the fact that surfing is a thrilling and enjoyable activity. If you see a break in your board, there is no need for alarm! The majority of cracks may be fixed at home as long as the affected region is cleaned, the resin is applied and cured correctly, and the board is sanded down.

Items You Need

- Rough grit sandpaper

- Plastic wrap

- UV resin

- Fine grit sandpaper

- Knife

- Q-Cell filler (optional)

- Application tool, such as a wooden spatula or spoon

- Fiberglass sheet (optional)

Part 1-Cleaning the Damaged Area

1-Wipe the board with a moist cloth to remove any wax, salt, or sand that may have accumulated on it.

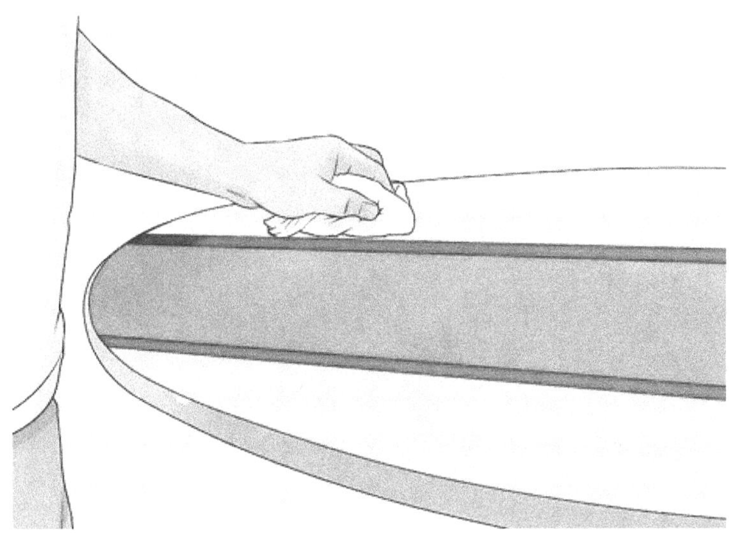

It is necessary to clean the board before attempting to make any repairs. To remove any sand, salt, or board wax from the surface, just use a towel and clean water to wash it off. Pay specific attention to the area surrounding the crack, since this is where board wax tends to accumulate. To remove any debris from the fracture, use a cotton swab.

- Any debris that is left within or around the fracture has the potential to get trapped in the resin, which will make the repair less effective.

**2-Allow the board to air dry for the whole
night**.

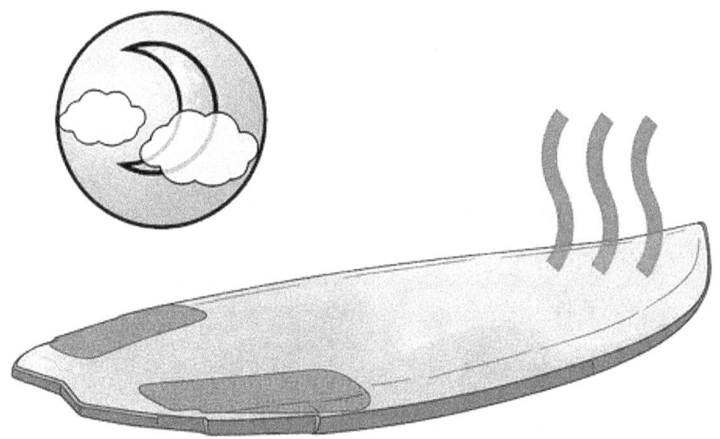

Placing the board in the open air and allowing it
to dry fully will prevent the repair glue from
absorbing moisture and fostering the growth of
mold. After a minimum of six hours, check to see
whether the board has dried out, and then
examine the crack. Before you start working, give
the crack a good push to make sure there is no
water escaping.

- Before commencing your repairs, you should wait for the crack to cure for an additional one to two days if it is still damp or if the board feels heavier in that particular place.

3-Remove any moldy foam from the interior of the crack using the utility knife.

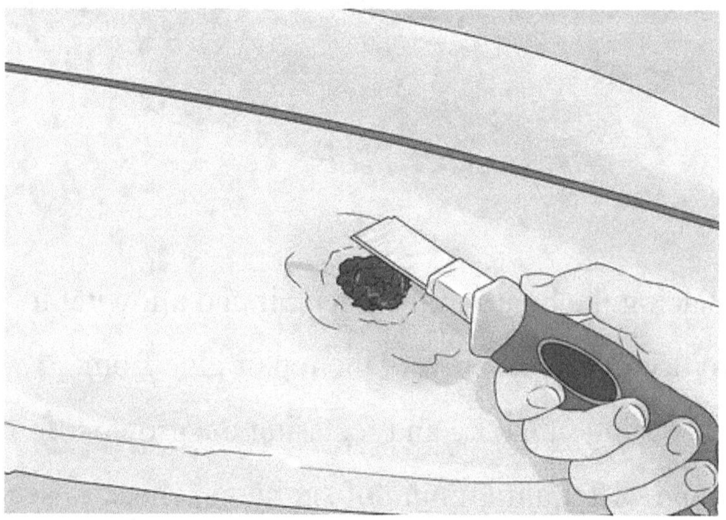

If your board has been cracked for an extended period of time or if a significant amount of water has entered the crack, the foam on the inside of your board may be rotten. Look for a brown or black foam that is pliable and has a pleasant feel.

Make cuts through the foam in a straight line with a sharp knife, and then throw away any moldy foam that you remove from the foam.

- Shine a light into the fissure if you are having trouble seeing the foam. In a normal situation, the color of the foam that is contained within the board will be visible to the naked eye.

4-Using sandpaper with a coarse grit, sand the crack until you reach the fiberglass cloth.

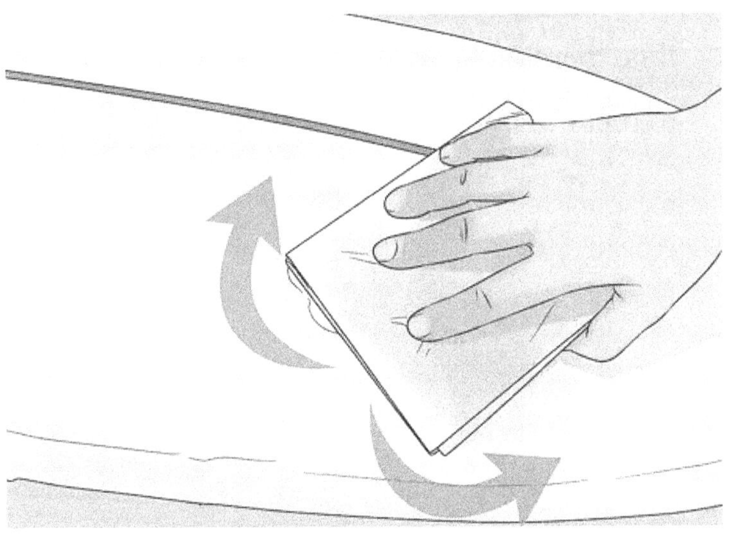

Sand an area that is slightly larger than the crack in the board using a rough piece of sandpaper and rubbing it over the crack in the board. Sanding should be stopped as soon as the fiberglass cloth that lies underneath the board's outer coating can be seen.

- Sanding a larger area is important because you want to blend the resin in with the surface of the board, so you need to make sure that you cover a large enough area. If you don't do this, there's a chance that you'll only be able to repair a portion of the crack.

Part 2-Putting The Resin Into Place

1-Obtain UV resin by shopping for it in a surf shop.

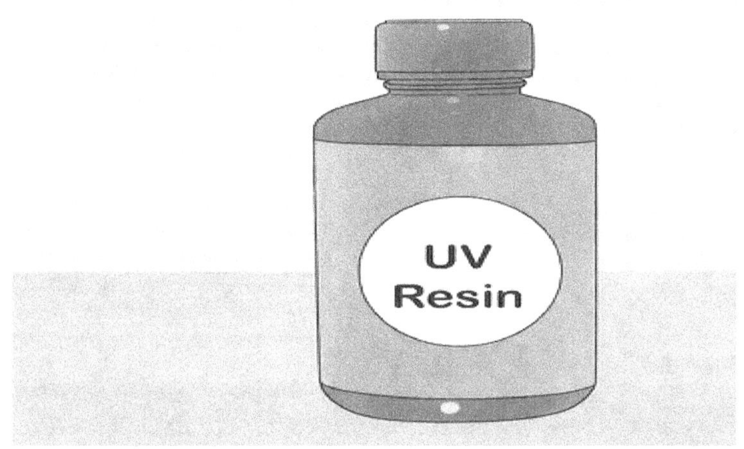

UV resin is an excellent choice for making quick fixes or smaller repairs. It is a liquid when it is first created, but once it is exposed to the light, it dries into a solid substance. Before beginning your repairs, you should look for the resin either online or in the surf shop that is closest to you.

● UV resin can withstand the majority of common surfing dings and cracks for a period of two to three months. After that, you will need to either do further repairs on the board or have it fixed by a professional.

2-To replace moldy foam, create a combination of resin and Q-Cell filler and stir it together.

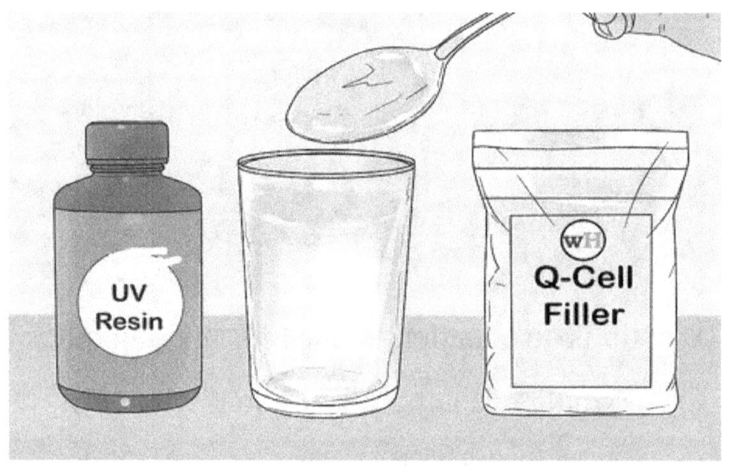

Because it grows in volume as it dries, Q-Cell filler may successfully take the place of foam in many applications. Put one fluid ounce or thirty milliliters of resin into a cup, and then gradually add Q-Cell filler to the resin until the mixture has the consistency of toothpaste.

- You may get Q-Cell filler from online sellers like as Amazon or eBay, or you can find it at most surf shops. Q-Cell filler is widely available.

- When starting off, use 2–3 fluid ounces (59–89 mL) of resin. This is the recommended amount to use when the crack is quite big or when you eliminated a lot of bad foam.

3-Apply resin generously all over the crack using a wooden stick or a spoon as a spreader.

First, in a shaded and protected place, squeeze some of the resin into the crack, and then use the remaining resin to fill in and smooth out the crack. Check to see that the resin is making contact with the board's outside shell. As you work, you should strive to pop any bubbles that develop in the resin as they appear.

- On the surface of the resin, you should strive to make it as smooth as possible, but you shouldn't be concerned if there are a few minor lumps.

4-Cover the resin with plastic wrap in order to keep it from moving while you work.

After the resin has been applied, proceed to cover the crack with a piece of plastic wrap and wrap the board in the wrap. This will keep the resin in place as it hardens and also shape it so that it conforms to the overall contours of the board.

- It is important to avoid pushing on the plastic wrap after it has been placed on the board since doing so will damage the resin before it has a chance to cure.

- In the event that you do not have any plastic wrap, you may use a standard piece of transparent plastic and attach it to the board.

5-Let the resin soak up the sun's rays for five to ten minutes.

Place the board in direct sunlight to hasten the curing of the resin. After five minutes, it will first transform into a gel and then become more solid.

Allow it to stay out in the sun for a further five minutes so that it may thoroughly solidify.

- If after 10 minutes the resin has not cured, put it in the shade for five minutes, and then bring it back into the light.

1-Give the resin a full night to dry out entirely.

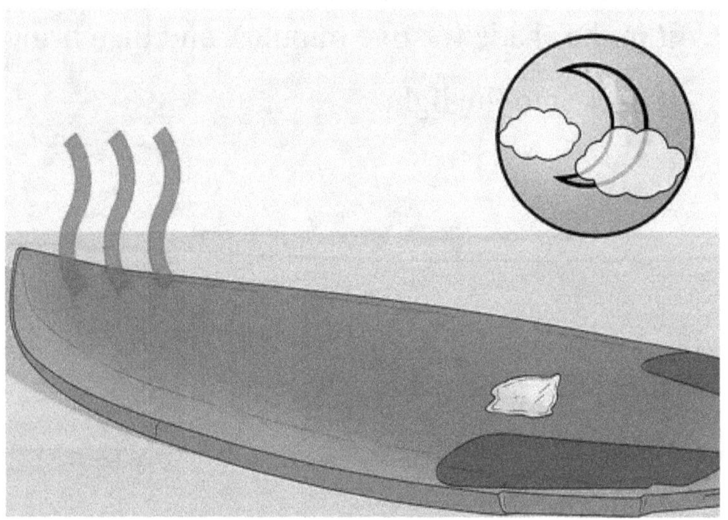

However, despite its brittle appearance, the resin has not yet lost all of its moisture. During the time that it is curing, you shouldn't touch either the plastic covering or the cracked region. Before removing the plastic wrap, you should first let it remain undisturbed for at least 6 to 12 hours.

● Some resins need air to set. Check the instructions that are printed on the package,

and if it says to do so, remove the plastic wrap
from the product before allowing it to cure.

**2-Remove any extra resin by sanding it down
until it is level with the board.**

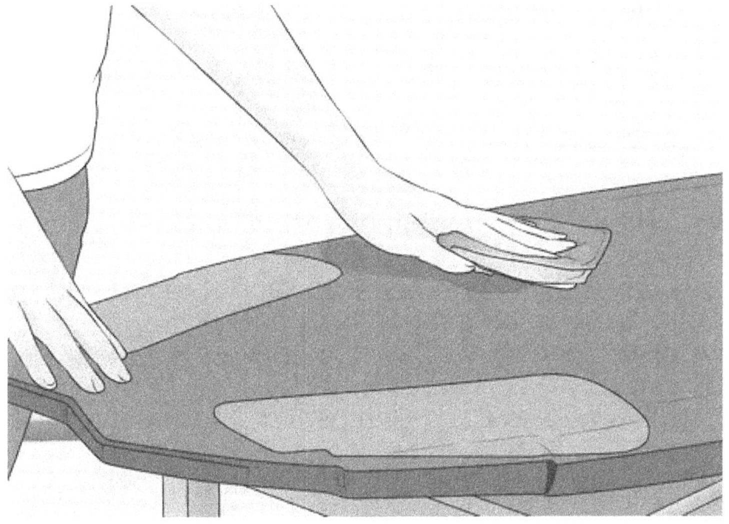

Sanding the resin using sandpaper that has a
coarse grain will eliminate the bigger lumps and
defects in the resin first. After that, go to a finer
grit in order to smooth out the resin so that it is
consistent with the board. After the resin has been
buffed to a smooth finish, remove any remaining

debris with a damp cloth and check that the resin's perimeters are flat with the rest of the board.

- You may find that you need to smooth the edges of the resin a little bit more in order to guarantee that it lies flat on the board and does not have any waves or bumps in it.

- When using sandpaper with a coarse grit, you need to be cautious not to sand it too much. In order to stop divots from appearing in the resin once the big bumps have been smoothed out, you should move to a smoother grit.

3-For further durability, cover the base with a layer of fiberglass and resin.

If you are concerned that your board may continue to break in the same location, you can cover the crack with a sheet of fiberglass that has been cut into a circle that is slightly bigger than the crack itself. After that, spread a thin coating of resin all over the fiberglass sheet using a paintbrush.

- If your board has a lengthy crack, you may cover the whole length by cutting a few smaller circles and aligning them along the crack. This will cover the crack.

4-If you added a layer of fiberglass, the resin needs another round of curing and sanding.

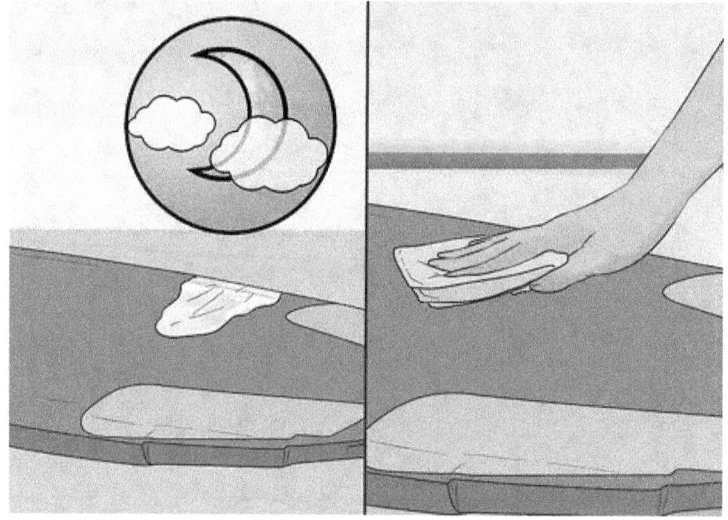

When the resin has been allowed to cure for a full 24 hours, you may use sandpaper with a very fine grain to smooth the resin out over the fiberglass. Sanding should continue until the surface of the board and the resin are completely flush with one another.

- Sandpaper with a very fine grain should only be used on fiberglass. A grit that is more aggressive may remove an excessive amount of resin, which can leave some of the fiberglass exposed.

www.ingramcontent.com/pod-product-compliance
Lightning Source LLC
Chambersburg PA
CBHW061702130726
47996CB00006B/2121